Adult Bullying

caring for yourself and others

"Stamping out bullying in the workplace and elsewhere is a vital objective. Not only can bullying make people's lives a misery, but it harms business and society too."

David Cameron

Adult Bullying

caring for yourself and others

Daniel Kearney

Published by Redemptorist Publications
Alphonsus House, Chawton, Hampshire, GU34 3HQ, UK
Tel: +44 (0)1420 88222, Fax: +44 (0)1420 88805
Email: rp@rpbooks.co.uk, www.rpbooks.co.uk

A registered charity limited by guarantee
Registered in England 3261721

Copyright © Redemptorist Publications 2017
First published November 2017

Series Editor: Sister Janet Fearns
Edited by Mandy Woods
Designed by Eliana Thompson

ISBN 978-0-85231-507-1

A CIP catalogue record for this book is available from the British Library.
The author would like to thank all those who have contributed to this book with the true
stories written in their own words.

The publisher gratefully acknowledges permission to use the following copyright material:
Excerpts from the *New Revised Standard Version Bible*: Anglicised Edition, copyright © 1989,
1995, Division of Christian Education of the National Council of the Churches of Christ in
the United States of America. Used by permission. All rights reserved.

Every effort has been made to trace copyright holders and to obtain their permission for the
use of copyright material. The publisher apologises for any errors or omissions and would
be grateful for notification of any corrections that should be incorporated in future reprints
or editions of this book.

Printed by Lithgo Press Ltd.,
Leicester, LE8 6NU

Introduction   1

1. How it feels to be bullied   3

2. Workplace bullying   7

3. For those who suffer   17

4. Adult bullying within the family   23

5. Others can help   29

6. For victims and those who care   33

7. In summary   47

8. Prayers and meditations   49

Introduction

Eradicating bullying from the workplace and elsewhere is a "vital objective" according to former prime minister David Cameron, and so we will need a strategic and all-inclusive approach to achieve this. If we can test and assess a business in terms of its productivity and financial health, then surely we can do the same when it comes to looking at how people in the workforce behave and interact with each other?

This book offers an alternative way of behaving in the workplace – a more virtuous and just way of managing people which is good for business and productivity and good for the workforce too.

It is a must-read for all business owners, managers and workers who aspire to put mutual respect, cooperation and transparency at the heart of their enterprise. It also helps clergy and pastoral workers to support parishioners who are victims of bullying and perhaps don't know what else they can do to call a halt to their suffering.

1

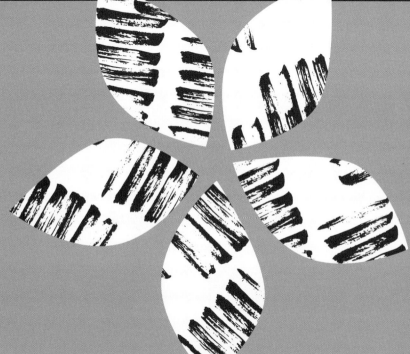

How it feels to be bullied

"I felt like a little whipped puppy cowering in the corner, expecting the next round of pain at any minute." Claire wept as she remembered her loss of confidence and self-esteem.

When younger, Mark, now a talented chef, suffered at the hands of someone who wanted his own skills to be recognised. "He insulted anything and everything I produced. In the end, I would only cook for myself, afraid to show others that I couldn't even boil an egg. That lasted for years."

Maria spoke at greater length. "Do you know how it feels to be bullied? It is like living in a cage. You can see through the bars and you long to fly but the door is padlocked and you don't have the key. You are a scared little bird with broken wings and an aching heart. You're scared and waiting to be humiliated even when nothing happens. You try to be extra nice to the bully, hoping that, on this occasion at least, you will succeed in bridging the gap between you. Your self-confidence is absolutely shattered. You tell yourself again and again that you are valuable; that you are gifted – that you are a human being. I can't put into words what it feels like to be reduced, by one person, to feeling subhuman, worthless and drowning. You repeatedly try to pick yourself up and to overcome the fear of being hurt yet again. You tell yourself that, on *this* occasion, you are going to be brave and stand up to the bully, but it doesn't work.

"What made me feel even worse was that other people seemed to be at ease in the bully's presence. Even I had to admit that she was basically a good person – but she picked on me and made my life a misery. The very best that I could do was never good enough – and yet I knew that her vindictiveness came from her own pain. I struggled to the best of my ability to be kind and compassionate. It didn't work.

"This situation continued for many years. People wouldn't believe me that this apparent paragon of virtue was actually a bully. They thought that there was something wrong with me, not with her. Why didn't I change jobs? I didn't have the courage: I mistakenly thought that it was only through kindness that my bosses had not sacked me. I thought I was so worthless as to be unemployable elsewhere. Yet now, when I look back on my achievements during those years, whatever I felt like inside, I actually did some amazing stuff. Had it not been for the bully, perhaps I might have achieved even more...

"These days, I don't know why, but the bullying has stopped. I've forgiven her but it's difficult to forget. Funnily enough, she has never realised how nasty she was and the damage she inflicted. I have no intention of taking revenge but it has taken me many years to rebuild my self-confidence. Surprisingly, I think I'm a better person for having been through the experience. I've learned the hard way to treat others with gentleness and respect so that they will not have to face everything that was a daily part of my own experience."

Ways of bullying

Bullies adopt different tactics in order to gain control of their victim, some of them subtle and others less so.

- The term "Stockholm syndrome" refers to the situation in which someone is taken captive and abused, yet eventually bonds with and becomes completely dependent on their captor. Fortunately this situation is rare. However, in less extreme situations, many victims describe going to extraordinary lengths to placate their bully. If someone seems unusually subservient and eager to please, it's worth asking if that person might be a victim of bullying.

- Verbal bullying is very common and hard to prove. It might include such things as repeatedly bringing up the victim's "silly mistakes", telling un-funny and belittling jokes, making snide comments or perhaps being just plain nasty. Does that sound familiar?

- Emotional bullying can involve a colleague being "accidentally on purpose" left out of an invitation to the pub for a drink after work, or making someone "invisible", for instance, in a staff meeting, where management seeks discussion but repeatedly ignores contributions from the victim. Rumours, broken confidences, background criticisms of work or appearance: all contribute to increasing the target's isolation and plummeting self-esteem.

- Sexual bullying occurs across gender differences – as shown in part of an overheard conversation between two gay men, where one said to the other, "You were really mean to me last night and I couldn't help crying." Sexual bullying need not be physical but it can be very intimidating nonetheless. So-called sexting, for example, is an increasingly common form of sexual bullying. And think of Fantine in *Les Misérables* as the factory supervisor pressurises her for sexual favours she refuses to give. Eventually he sacks her, blaming her for the disturbance on the factory floor when, in fact, he is punishing Fantine for rejecting his advances – but she could have kept her job had she agreed to sleep with him.

- Group bullies do not work alone. They need each other's support for maximum effect. They gang up on their intended victim, inflicting maximum pain simply because then the victim must deal with more than one person at a time. It's really tough when it feels to the victim as though "everyone" at work is focusing upon them, and it's not uncommon for someone in such a position to suffer a breakdown or even to take their own life.

- Indifference can feel particularly cruel. No matter how hard the victim tries to please the bully, their efforts count for nothing. There is never any sign of pleasure, not a word of thanks and no appreciation.

- Often, the bullying is that person's way of getting rid of pent-up anger and frustration, and they feel like a victim themselves. But as the saying goes, "God help the victim of the victim!"

- Cyberbullying is a form of bullying that is on the increase. It takes so little effort to send that nasty email, doesn't it?

2

Workplace bullying

Sadly, bullying in the workplace is a common scourge and it is as virulent as it is on the school playground. A recent headline in *The Times* newspaper declared: "Quarter of minority staff in NHS are bullied". The article commented that bullying was having a detrimental impact on patient care as bullied staff felt demotivated and fed up with what had become routine behaviour.

This illustrates the point that bullying affects everyone in some shape or form. It is not confined merely to the bully or to the victim. It is bad for business too. There is no teamwork if the so-called team leader is a bully. Instead, any achievements happen within an environment of fear, coercion and resentment: hardly conducive to friendship, cooperation and transparency.

Bullying and harassment

Bullying is not against the law, but **harassment,** which is often confused with bullying behaviour, is unlawful under the Equality Act 2010. It is important to be able to distinguish between the two.

Harassment is when unwanted behaviour is related to one of the following:

- Age
- Sex
- Disability
- Gender
- Marriage or civil partnership
- Pregnancy or maternity
- Race or nationality
- Religion or belief
- Sexual orientation

Margaret received regular harassment from another woman because of her nationality: "She repeatedly made disparaging remarks about my nationality and country, either to me personally or, pointedly, in my hearing. She said of Tess, a bereaved countrywoman of mine, 'She didn't even cry. That just goes to show what people from your country are like!' To be honest, I'd really admired Tess for her dignified coping with her mother's funeral."

Workplace bullying is a persistent pattern of mistreatment from others in the workplace, causing either physical or emotional harm. It can include such tactics as verbal, nonverbal, psychological and physical abuse and also humiliation.

Pat offered an example of her experience of being bullied: "My boss didn't speak to me for several days because we were independently invited to the same important event. He was furious that I could be there in my own right and he couldn't stop it."

The serial bully

Tim Field, who coined the phrase "serial bully" when he ran the UK National Workplace Bullying Advice Line, noted that, when called to account for their actions, serial bullies instinctively respond with **denial** and **retaliation** and by **feigning victimhood**. He described this as a deliberate, learned strategy with a clear purpose.

As with the school bully, the workplace bully is often someone who feels insecure, threatened or intimidated by another person in some way. In the workplace it might simply be because other people are excelling at their job and the bully is not and so they try to eliminate the competition to show they are better.

Some bullies appear in unexpected places – as Father Tony explains. "My problem is Maud, a battle-axe who controls the sacristy, the church, the parish – and the priests. My predecessor blamed her for the ulcer which caused his early retirement. I'm terrified of the woman. I hide when I see her coming but, sooner or later, I have no choice: I have to go into the church. Even there, she publicly controls the smallest details. It can be really embarrassing. Maud makes me feel like a naughty child. I'm sure that my constant headaches are because of her – but how do I get rid of her when she is an unpaid volunteer *and* a parishioner? She is even worse when the bishop comes, but is so careful of seeing to *his* every wish that *he* thinks she's wonderful. He listens to her complaints about me and tells *me* to be kinder and more sympathetic towards *her*. It's reached the stage when it's either Maud or me – and I've a horrible feeling that I'll be the one to go. I'm really sorry because I love this parish but I can no longer put up with Maud."

A serial bully could be anyone. Rather than using physical violence, the serial bully targets people with methods that are harder for onlookers to recognise. They use such tactics as abusing the authority that comes with their position, emotional blackmail, malicious gossip and one-on-one confrontations when there are no witnesses.

I remember from my own teaching career coming across many teachers who fell into the serial-bully category. One in particular sticks in my mind for the sheer ruthlessness with which she persecuted several victims over a number of years. Whenever a new teacher came into the department where the serial bully worked, the bully felt vulnerable and set about undermining their new colleague at every opportunity by spreading lies about them to pupils, to other colleagues and to parents. The whispering campaign was a constant hum within the department and throughout the school. Very little could ever be done to stop the intimidation and bullying because the bully was highly intelligent and covered her tracks so well. It was a constant source of frustration for management, having to replace staff every year as the bully saw off all competition.

The bullying teacher – what would you do in response?

a) Do whatever it takes to placate the bully and have a quiet life in your new job?

b) Take the bully on at her own game and spread counter-rumours and lies to pupils, parents and colleagues as she has done about you?

c) Resign from your position?

d) Try to resolve the issues through mediation and counselling?

Because the serial bully feels threatened by colleagues with competence, integrity and popularity, sooner or later they will identify a talented member of staff and project onto them their own inadequacy and incompetence. Using unwarranted criticism and threats, the serial bully controls them and subjugates them, without a thought for the valuable contribution that person makes to the organisation. The bully totally disregards their victim's self-esteem, self-confidence, loyalty and health. Sooner or later this person – the bully's "target" – realises that they are now being bullied. When this realisation becomes apparent to the bully, sensing that the target might complain to a higher authority and expose their misconduct, the bully neutralises the target by isolating them and destroying their credibility and reputation among decision-makers and peers, and then putting them out of the picture through dismissal, forced resignation or even early retirement. Once the target has gone, within about two weeks, the serial bully's focus turns to someone else and the cycle starts again.

Christina commented, "My boss didn't know how to deal with women who had a similar level of education and expertise. He made my life very difficult. Before I left my job he employed a very young woman to do most of my work. It was very pointed, especially as she was newly qualified, and had little experience and even less basic general knowledge. He could bully her. She didn't last long."

Recognisable character traits of a serial bully are:

- having a Jekyll and Hyde nature – Dr Jekyll is charming and charismatic; Hyde is evil;

- being a convincing liar – the serial bully makes up anything to fit his needs at that moment and is believed;

- treating some people in a way that causes them unprecedented levels of stress, frustration and fear;

- damaging the reputations of organisations and individuals, as well as the health of the latter;

- reacting to criticism with denial and retaliation and by feigning victimhood and blaming the real victims;

- being apparently immune from disciplinary action;

- moving to a new target when the present one burns out or leaves.

Ricky commented, "I tried telling a mutual friend about the bullying I was receiving at work, but he didn't believe me. He supported my boss and severed all further communication with me. I had nobody else to whom I could turn and so the bullying continued."

Such cases are not unique but do highlight the difficulty in rooting out many bullies who know and play the system to their advantage, often complaining about any intervention and kicking up a stink at the merest suggestion that they might be a bully.

Bullies instinctively deny any allegation made. Sometimes the denial is direct and robust. Sometimes it involves avoiding discussion of the matter that has been raised, never giving a straight answer, deliberately missing the point and creating distractions and diversions. Variations include trivialisation of the concern, and offering the target a "clean slate" or a "fresh start". Where a person targeted has hinted at their dissatisfaction with a serial bully's conduct towards them, they can expect to hear:

- This is so trivial it's not worth talking about, and I'm not going to discuss it.

- It is my job to manage you. No one else has complained.

- I don't know why you're so intent on dwelling on the past.

- Look, what's past is past, I'll overlook the very serious accusations you've made and we'll start afresh.

As well as being a form of denial, this false conciliation is an abdication of responsibility for any damage done. This approach may be effective in a workplace in the short term but it does not (or should not) work in court, where the problem for the target, and the advantage for the bully, is that reliving the conversation in a courtroom environment is literally years away from this unmoderated discussion at work. The best thing a person who is being bullied can do in this situation is to keep accurate notes of the response to their allegation, since a serial bully can probably out-talk anyone who argues with them.

All too often the serial bully makes counter-allegations and, in many cases, being shrewd and streetwise, they have plausible evidence to support their claims, which they have carefully collated knowing, from past experience, that an allegation will, at some point, inevitably be levelled against them. They might, in their defence, claim:

- I'm the one being bullied here.
- I am deeply offended.
- If it were not for me, you would not be so fortunate/wouldn't have your job/wouldn't have been promoted etc.
- You don't know how hard it is for me.
- I'm the one who's under stress.
- You think you're having a hard time....
- After all I/we have done for you....
- Etc. etc.

Feigned victimhood, as this is known, can include bursting into tears (which is guaranteed to make the other person uncomfortable and to lead to a comfort break or even an end to the discussion), displays of indulgent self-pity, pretending to be indignant or to feel "devastated" or "deeply offended", being histrionic, playing the martyr and generally trying to make others feel sorry for them – a "poor me" melodrama.

This has certainly been my experience of dealing with a serial bully.

"The hardest challenge is to be yourself in a world where everyone is trying to make you be someone else."

E.E. Cummings

The adult bully

Megan looked stunned. The young woman was genuinely surprised. "Do you mean to say that grown-ups get bullied?" Her two middle-aged companions smiled sadly. "Unfortunately, yes" – and said no more. They didn't have to. Each suddenly realised that the other had spoken from personal experience.

It is important to note that there is little you can do about an adult bully, other than to ignore them and, if it is happening at work, try to avoid them after reporting the abuse to a supervisor. This is because adult bullies often operate in a set pattern. They are not interested in working things out and they are not interested in compromise. Rather, adult bullies are more interested in power and domination. They want to feel as though they are important and preferred, and they accomplish this by bringing others down. Because such bullies are so fundamentally and psychologically damaged that there are no strategies, short of instant dismissal, that will ever bear fruit.

For a whole host of psychological and emotional problems and issues, such people must exert their dominance over others. If a colleague is perceived by them to be more popular, achieves better exam results or is better at different things, in their mind this exposes their own inadequacies, and the colleague then becomes the target of their anger. For example, if a colleague's work practices differ from theirs, this can undermine the bully's perceived authority and control.

In short, unless their target is subservient and conforms absolutely to how the bully wants them to behave, there will always be conflict. Any deviation from the bully's wishes is seen as a challenge and threat to his or her world view and way of doing things.

Generally, adult bullies fall into the following categories:

- A **narcissistic bully** has no empathy for other human beings. This individual may find pleasure in another person's pain.

- An **impulsive bully** does not mastermind his or her bullying attempts. This person may simply grow angry and not have a better way to handle such anger.

- A **physical bully** either threatens physical abuse or eventually uses physical abuse.

- A **verbal bully** often uses demeaning, vulgar or persecutory words to insult the receiver of their email or website messages.

- A **secondary bully** is a person who does not initially start the bullying, but joins in. He or she may get a dysfunctional pleasure from picking on someone who is seen as weak by a friend.

- Finally, a **workplace bully** is a manager or a co-worker who bullies by spreading rumours, taunting the victim, or forcing him or her to engage in activities that he or she may not want to perform. Sexual harassment often occurs because of workplace bullies.

"Bullying is for people who have no confidence at all. So everyone being bullied please remember they are scared of you. You have something they don't, and that's what makes them bully you. Don't let their words affect you because they are the ones needing confidence, not you."

Anonymous

3

For those who suffer

"Never be bullied into silence. Never allow yourself to be made a victim. Accept no one's definition of your life; define yourself."

Harvey Fierstein

For those who suffer from bullying in the workplace, it is a debilitating and traumatic experience. It corrodes confidence and ripples out far beyond the workplace to affect all facets of the victim's life, family and relationships. It saps energy and motivation and often results in depression and, tragically, sometimes in suicide.

There are some differences between adult and childhood bullying. Often the adult victim feels powerless, ashamed and guilt-ridden. Because bullying is "not supposed to happen to adults" – it is something associated in most people's minds with the playground only – it may be difficult for them to find someone who is prepared to listen and offer advice.

There are, however, similarities between those bullied at school and those bullied in the workplace. The *Annual Bullying Survey for 2016* listed the following reasons why children are bullied, but the list applies to many adults too:

- Physical appearance
- Race and/or ethnicity
- Sexual orientation
- Religious denomination
- Disabilities or speech impediments
- Behaviour and mannerisms
- Background
- Educational needs

Bullying is behaviour that is repeated, often on a daily basis and, in most cases, over a long period of time. According to the late anti-bullying activist Tim Field, "Bullying consists of the least competent, most aggressive employee projecting their incompetence on the least aggressive, most competent employee and winning." In the workplace, this often manifests itself in the bully excluding their target from work-related social events, giving them the "silent treatment", refusing to help them with tasks, and spreading malicious rumours and lies about them among other workers or on social media. Those who are being bullied often go through a whole range of emotions during this process. They may:

- feel guilty and that it's their own fault, so they deserve it;
- feel ashamed of themselves for not having the strength or the courage to stand up to the bully;
- feel rejected, useless, worthless;
- feel hopeless, despairing, suicidal.

What can be done?

Despite the trauma and difficulties associated with being bullied, there are things that can be done.

Many people try to address the problem personally before taking official steps to put an end to the situation that is making their life a misery. Much can often be achieved without recourse to union representatives, employment tribunals and the full force of employment legislation.

It is important to recognise that a strategy which helps one individual might not offer a solution to someone else, simply because of personality differences. Whereas one victim might be able to use humour to defuse an event, not everybody can crack a joke when they feel threatened. Simply walking away while the bully is mid-sentence might be a less stressful option: nothing needs to be said and the bully is the one who looks foolish, talking to thin air. Similarly, if the threat comes via a telephone call, merely replace the receiver. There is no need to listen to the end of the tirade.

The following are some strategies tried by different individuals with some measure of success:

- Jamie, a young graduate, found temporary work as a gardener while he looked for a permanent position. "My line manager told me to sweep up the fallen leaves, dump them on the compost heap and not to come indoors until I'd finished. An increasingly strong wind made the task impossible. Although it was already dark, he refused my request to abandon the job for the night and continue the following day in daylight and, hopefully, without the wind. A few minutes later, I downed tools anyway and went indoors. My line manager could say nothing: everyone had seen the bullying and was quietly glad that someone had stood up to him."

- Morag was too afraid of her line manager to verbally defend herself. "When my line manager heard that my bosses had unexpectedly offered me my dream job, he responded with (yet another) string of verbal abuse. Although shaking with fear, I walked out of the office whilst he was still speaking. Two similar episodes of nastiness followed, but again, I just left the office without saying anything. I felt stronger for it. I'd learned that I did not have to be the victim: I could choose to leave a painful situation. My line manager could do nothing because our bosses had approved my new role." Although fear kept Morag from speaking up for herself, silently walking away from the tirade protected her and left her line manager without a victim.

- Sandy tried something else: "After many years of being bullied, my self-confidence had reached zero. I printed out a picture of Alice in Wonderland saying, 'You're nothing but a pack of cards!' and kept it in my pocket. Whenever the bully came anywhere near me, I thought to myself, 'You're nothing but a pack of cards!' I gradually stopped being scared, learned to handle her outbursts and the bullying stopped."

- Beth finally plucked up the courage she needed to defend herself: "I made a silly mistake when I was young. Twenty-six years later, the bully would still tell complete strangers about my mistake, joking about it in my presence. One day, I decided I'd had enough. Although I was scared, I said, "That happened many years ago and is no longer funny." Since then, I've never heard the story repeated. The bully was used to browbeating people who had not been able to challenge his behaviour."

- Tony also managed to find his voice. "A colleague repeatedly criticised me over anything and everything. One day I turned to him and said that perhaps my work was almost as poor as his. He hadn't expected me to stand up for myself and to challenge his own performance in the workplace. Following a couple of similar episodes when I spoke up, life has become much more peaceful. I learned that it can pay to refuse to become the victim of a bully. I was really scared the first time I spoke up and half-expected him to hit me. I couldn't believe it when he almost melted and suddenly acted with courtesy. I quickly walked away, my heart still pounding, but feeling unbelievably good about myself."

- Anne focused, in her spare time, on her strengths. "I've written since I could hold a pencil. Writing is in my DNA. Unknown to the person who bullied me for years, writing became my salvation and my release from her control. She could not stop me doing something I love. I felt that she lost control over me whenever I sat down to write: it was something I could do and she couldn't. I love writing. I love doing the background research. I love using words as building blocks in order to create something which, an hour or so earlier, had not existed. I love selecting, arranging and placing each word in just the right place so that the final result gives joy to myself and others. I write and I'm as free as a bird: this was something that the bully could not take away from me. Today publishers use almost everything I write – and the bully is nowhere to be seen."

When official support is needed

Sometimes, however, it feels as though nothing works, and in those situations official support is needed.

Employees who feel that they are being bullied should initially speak to someone within the organisation or company who can help – for example, a human resources (HR) officer or union representative. They can make a formal complaint using their employer's grievance procedure. If this does not work and they are still being bullied or harassed they can take their case to an employment tribunal.

There are agencies that can help with bullying in the workplace, such as ACAS (Advisory, Conciliation and Arbitration Service – 0300 123 1100) and the National Bullying Helpline (0845 22 55 787 or 07734 701221). Most experts will suggest at least some of the following strategies to help immediately or in the short term:

- Avoid the bully or bullies whenever possible but do not make your avoidance too obvious as it might be seen as a sign of weakness.

- Try to ignore inappropriate behaviour – don't rise to the bait.

- Try to use humour to defuse the situation – take the sting out of the bully.

- Remain calm and confident, and try to be assertive but not aggressive. Document any offences, keeping an up-to-date record of all bullying behaviour, as well as times, dates, places and possible witnesses.

- Speak to someone who might help – for example, the HR officer, the union representative or someone in senior management. After such a meeting always send a follow-up email or letter outlining what was discussed and the help and advice offered.

- Try not to take the bully's behaviour to heart. The problem is with them, not you.

- Never get physical or reciprocate with bullying behaviour of your own.

4

Adult bullying within the family

Paul arrived at the A&E department of the local hospital bleeding heavily from his mouth. "My son is a drug addict and always comes home when he runs out of cash. I came in from work and found him going through the drawers in the bedroom. I told him I had no money to give him, but he turned round and started hitting me. Yes, my mouth hurts, but what hurts more is that he is my son and he did this."

Bullying within the family can be particularly painful, especially because the family is meant to be a place of safety. There is the added factor that both the bully and the victim may love each other dearly. Yet, instead of trying to create a loving, supportive, secure environment for every member of the family, the bully can be an expert at setting one person against another, using emotional blackmail and manipulation, and controlling friends and visitors to the house, as well as the finances, work, movement... Elderly or sick relatives, the vulnerable and the young can become targets. Male bullies tend not to be subtle and might be prone to using physical means, including violence, whereas female bullies tend to be more subtle and use manipulation to get what they want.

Helpful strategies for handling the adult family bully can include the following:

- Avoid becoming emotional. Stay calm. You might be unable to control the bully but you can control your reaction. This might be all you need to defuse the situation.

- Stop blaming yourself. You did not ask to be bullied. You are not the problem.

- Remain confident. Even if you are scared inside, avoid looking nervous, insecure or defeated. The family bully will quickly identify whom they can manipulate and control.

- Try holding a frank and honest discussion, either on a one-to-one basis, as a family group or facilitated through an independent third party.

- Plan your responses ahead of time, perhaps even using a mirror.

- Use such phrases as "I think..." or "I feel..." rather than "You do..." or "You are...", which might antagonise the bully and cause an argument.

- Try looking the bully straight in the eye and saying, "Excuse me?"

- Remove yourself from the situation. Find somewhere private (the bathroom?), go for a walk – do whatever you need to do to give yourself time to de-stress and the bully time to cool down.

- When you have some quiet time and space, think about what you could do differently next time a difficult situation arises relating to the bully.

- Know when to look for outside help.

- If the situation becomes so hard that there is a threat to life and limb, you might have to consider the possibility of moving out.

Peter, a victim of bullying over a prolonged period, realised he had to do something when a seemingly trivial decision reduced him to a quivering jelly at the thought of possible consequences for making an incorrect choice: "We had two tea caddies to separate two different types of tea. One evening, finding an empty caddy, I went to refill it and went into a blind panic because I couldn't remember which tea went into which caddy. I felt literally sick with fear of the possible consequences. I decided that this was crazy. Whatever the consequences, a packet of tea was not going to destroy my life. I put the tea into the caddy I had in my hand – and nobody noticed. From that moment, I started to take my life back into my hands and to make decisions once again. I began, gradually, to feel my self-confidence return."

Mita came in to work with yet another black eye after, yet again, apparently walking into a door at home. Her employers helped her to find a house where she could live with other women. It was not an officially designated "safe house" but, for Mita, that is exactly what it became. Her husband could no longer bully her. Within a short time, she was a smiling, peaceful, confident woman. If she had stayed with her husband, she would have remained nervous, grim and unhappy – or even worse. There are some circumstances when separation can mean the difference between being able to live a normal life and coming to potentially serious harm.

Elderly parents

Elderly parents can be both the bullied and the bullies, in both cases creating anxiety and heartache for those who love them.

Elderly bullies

When elderly parents become the bullies, the cause often arises from their own frustration at growing older and gradually losing their earlier independence and control. Unfortunately, family members are often the easiest targets and take the brunt of parental anger, feeling unable to stand up for themselves and ill-equipped to identify strategies. There can also be a sense of disloyalty and betrayal if children – even as adults – seek help and advice outside the family.

The following ideas might help:

- Don't take the bullying and insults personally. Although you might be the victim, the anger and bullying are because your mum or dad is probably frustrated with the direction in which their own life is heading. You just happen to be the nearest soft target for them to vent that disappointment.

- Don't treat your parent as though he or she is a child who needs to be told what to do and when to do it. Check with them as to what their needs actually are.

- Give yourself a breathing space. Go out for a walk. Meet up with a friend for a coffee.

- Talk with other caregivers: you will probably find that your problems are actually quite common. You are not alone. This is a shared and common situation. Although talking doesn't remove the pain and anxiety, venting your own feelings in a safe environment can give you the courage and strength you need to go back into the arena. It can be a huge support to learn that you are not the only family member to be in the firing line.

- Don't feel guilty for trying to tell your parent that you deserve better treatment than you are receiving from them.

- Sometimes you have to lay down the law regardless of the anger that might result: there comes a time when an elderly person should no longer be driving and is a risk to themselves and others. However, before taking away the keys, try to come to an agreement about driving less frequently or only in daylight and to places nearby.

- Mail-order catalogues are a potential nightmare and can lead to unnecessary expenditure. Contact the companies sending them to your parent and, where possible, quietly insist that their name is taken off the mailing list. If you act quietly in the background, it avoids anger.

Elderly victims

As people age and gradually let go of their earlier abilities and independence, younger family members can sometimes become bullies, causing needless distress and suffering for a parent or grandparent. If something doesn't feel right in terms of the way you are being treated, it probably isn't. You don't have to put up with it.

The following strategies might help:

- Remember that you are not a child who needs to be told what to do and when to do it.

- Don't be pressurised into handing out money.

- Consider taking out a Power of Attorney so that there is support available should you need it but you still have an agreed level of autonomy.

- Talk with your children about how all of you would like to be treated and search together for solutions to issues involving such things as medication, finance, stairs, safety alarms, hygiene and so on.

- Agree personal boundaries: you can do some things for yourself, while you may need help for others.

- Define limits to taking responsibility for looking after your grandchildren: all day every day is probably more than you can reasonably handle.

- Don't put up with:
    - being touched in ways that make you uncomfortable;
    - decision-making about you without your involvement;
    - being made to feel small or threatened;
    - physical hurt;
    - neglect;
    - hunger;
    - withholding of medical care and/or medication.

- Know how to contact your doctor, social services and even, should it become necessary, the police.

5

Others can help

We all have a role to play in combatting bullying. The act of bullying does not just involve the bully and their victim. It is highly likely that most people will have witnessed acts of bullying in their lives, either at school or in the workplace. If we stand by and allow the bullying to continue then we are condoning it and giving the bully an audience. But how should we respond, particularly if we fear the bully might turn his attention on us too?

Whether you know the person being bullied or not, there are dos and don'ts that you, as a bystander, can take on board to support them:

- Don't laugh and join in.

- Don't encourage the bully in any way.

- Don't video the bullying.

- Stay at a safe distance and help the victim get away.

- Write down everything you have seen and heard. This will be really helpful in enabling others to gain an understanding of what has been going on.

- Don't become an "audience" for the bully.

- Reach out to the victim in friendship.

- Help and support the victim in any way you can.

- If you notice someone being deliberately isolated from others, invite them to join you.

- Tell a manager, supervisor or someone in higher authority than the bully.

Such strategies are sound and in many situations might help to resolve the issue, but they do not tackle the underlying causes of bullying, either in school, in the workplace or in a relationship. Something more radical is required, something more profound than merely dealing with the symptoms or trying to minimise the effects bullying has on both those who bully and those who are bullied. It tarnishes and spoils both.

Pause for thought

The presence of bullying in our lives, in our relationships and in our places of education and work should call upon all of us to reflect on the following aspects of our lives:

- the type of person we want to be or to become;

- the nature of the relationships we want with others as well as with ourself;

- the nature of the society, community, workplace or family we want to live in and to contribute to in a positive and affirming way.

It is only by undergoing such rigorous self-searching and self-analysis that we might, as individuals and as members of society, be able to prevent bullying even if we are not able to eradicate it altogether from our lives.

Start with me

"My mother bullied me all my life. She now lives in a care home. She doesn't know that every time I give her Communion, whilst, aloud, I say, 'The Body of Christ' and wait for her 'Amen', in my heart, I deliberately say, 'I forgive you'. She doesn't know that and it makes no difference to her life – but it changes mine. I believe that, with God's help, my wanting to forgive will no longer be simply an intellectual exercise: it will gradually work its way down to my heart."

The starting point must always be ourselves. We can't change another person but we can show them, by personal example and witness, a different and a more self-fulfilling way of living. We can offer them a way to form positive and healthy relationships with other people. But we can only draw close to people who believe, think and act differently from us if we have something better to offer them. To do this requires a vision, a unifying shape of how to live and how to treat others. In an increasingly secularised world, and with so many competing truths and lifestyles to contend with, this might seem to be an impossible task.

It is essential that in any episodes of bullying or harassment the spotlight is shone on the bully, not on their victim, because the problem originates with the bully. What need to be exposed are the unresolved issues and conflicts which plague the bully and not whether or not the victim is too sensitive or too meek to stand up to such behaviour. By tormenting someone else, the bully reveals something about their own inner self-dislike, insecurity and inadequacies; something they see in the victim which they envy and would like to be themselves.

As we have seen, being the victim of bullying can often cause a person to become introspective and to feel and believe that they are in some way responsible for eliciting such attention. It is "their fault" and they "deserve" to be treated in this way because they are "weak" and "useless".

It is worth reiterating again and again that the problem lies with the bully and not with the victim. But when one is at the sharp end of bullying behaviour this can be difficult to remember. Bullies turn the victim's world upside down, and what seems straightforward and obviously wrong to those on the outside might not be so clear-cut and apparent to the victim. In the maelstrom of emotions and fear the victim often loses all sense of proportion. Bullies thrive on such dislocation and emotional upheaval.

6

For victims and those who care

"Each of us deserves the freedom to pursue our own version of happiness. No one deserves to be bullied."

Barack Obama

Those who pick up the pieces and try to rebuild the self-esteem and self-confidence of the victim will first have to chip away patiently at the layers of abuse and suffering the victim might have endured before revealing they are being, or have been, bullied. This is by no means an easy task. But there is a way forward, a roadmap for the journey.

Catholic theology in the past put great faith in the four so-called cardinal virtues – prudence, courage, temperance and justice. The Latin word *virtus* literally means "strength", and these four cardinal virtues can help us to be strong when dealing with the trials and tribulations of being bullied. The virtues give us the ability and constancy to be good and to achieve good in our lives and in the lives of others. The word "cardinal" derives from the Latin word for "hinge" because all other virtues hinge on these four cardinal virtues. Without the virtues of prudence, courage, temperance and justice we have no reliable moral compass to guide us through life. We are all at sea, directionless. Let us look at each in turn and examine how they might help us.

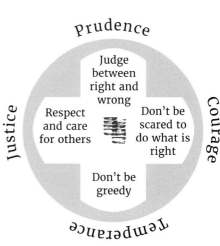

prudence

Judge between right and wrong

Justice — Respect and care for others

Courage — Don't be scared to do what is right

Don't be greedy

Temperance

33

The virtue of prudence – *this virtue allows us to judge correctly what is right and wrong in any given situation.*

Bullies will invariably attempt to rationalise and normalise their behaviour. In defence of their bullying behaviour, they often claim to be the victim themselves, and most are captivating and convincing in this role! Remember that they are arch-manipulators of people, situations, truth and facts. They can all too easily make their victim think and feel it's their fault, that they are the one to blame for being bullied.

But bullies feel threatened by colleagues who exhibit competence, integrity and popularity, and so, in a calculated attempt to remain in control, they often project their own inadequacies and incompetence onto those they target as their victims. This can have a deeply dislocating and emotionally disorientating effect on the victim. It turns their world, seemingly, upside down and leads them to question their own understanding and judgement of the situation. Such sinister shifting of the moral compass is precisely what the bully wishes to achieve because the finger of blame is now pointing at the so-called victim and not at the bully. The bully then takes absolute and cruel control and coldly neutralises the target by isolating them and, finally, by destroying their credibility and reputation. At this point, in a work setting, the victim either capitulates or resigns.

Critically at such times, amid all the hullaballoo and emotional upheaval and stress churned up by the bully's actions, it is our ability to judge correctly for ourselves what is right and what is wrong – to be able to take a step back from the precipice and to see objectively what is actually happening – that will keep us sane and safe. The virtue of prudence enables us to do just that. It keeps our moral compass true and steadfast amid all the turmoil and false readings of the fray. But being in tune with our moral soundings and knowing how to exercise prudence is something which we have to work at. Although like a migratory instinct it is hard-wired within our make-up, like most things which are good and true, it takes time and effort to hone it to our advantage. But when it is working for our benefit, it is an indispensable and reliable part of our moral armour. It affords us the security and confidence to know for certain what in any given situation is right and what is not right, in spite of how the bully might try to manipulate and misrepresent the reality of the situation.

I recall a situation where the virtue of prudence was very much in evidence in a newly qualified language teacher. She was, she believed, being bullied by her head of department, but experienced colleagues in the department dismissed her as "over sensitive" and her worries and concerns as being "exaggerated". But the young teacher persisted with her belief and, as it transpired, she was indeed correct in her conviction. Her moral compass had been true and pointing in the right and proper direction. She was being bullied, but in such a subtle and sinister way that even experienced and decent colleagues had missed it. The bully in this case appeared, on the surface, to be plausible, but under scrutiny the Dr Jekyll patina quickly disappeared and Mr Hyde soon appeared. Even in the face of overwhelming evidence the bully continued in her denial, which is a characteristic of the serial bully. There is all too often, regrettably, a tendency in many places of work to side with experience over youth in such instances of alleged bullying, but this particular case involving the young language teacher certainly taught me an invaluable lesson in dealing with such matters.

In the workplace so many excuses are made for this unacceptable behaviour, ranging from "it's just his robust management style" to a workshop foreman claiming "it's just a bit of banter" when offensive homophobic comments are directed at team members.

As Rosaria, who was bullied by her supervisor as a young cleaner, commented, "She was always criticising my work, telling me that I hadn't cleaned rooms which I'd just cleaned from top to bottom. I was so scared of her. In the end, whenever I had finished with a room, I sprayed inside every cupboard with air freshener as proof that I had been there. I'm pretty sure she never checked any of my work because nothing was ever said about the air freshener in the cupboards. When I complained about her, I was told that she was going through 'a difficult time' and 'that's the way she is with youngsters'. I'm sorry, but nearly thirty years later, she still never bothers even to greet me when we meet in the street. She was a bully and I breathed a sigh of relief when I was assigned to a different supervisor."

The virtue of courage/fortitude – *this virtue allows us to overcome fear and to remain steady in our will in the face of trials and tribulations.*

"You have enemies?" enquired Winston Churchill. "Good. That means you've stood up for something." The young language teacher certainly stood up for something – for truth and for decency – and in doing so she displayed the virtue of courage in her conviction that she was being bullied when others had dismissed and downplayed her concerns. She demonstrated great fortitude in persevering and in trusting her instincts and judgement. Standing up to a bully, particularly one who might be physically more imposing or in a higher position of authority than you, can be a daunting and fearful experience for most people. In such circumstances it is worth recalling Benjamin Disraeli's quote about bullying: "courage is fire, and bullying is smoke".

In most instances a bully will back down in the face of a courageous but not confrontational person. In their world only might is right and has the upper hand, but if you can steal their thunder then you can turn the tables on them.

An incident related to me by a colleague illustrates this well. He had just been appointed, at a relatively young age, to the position of headmaster at an independent school on the verge of bankruptcy. On his first day in office a long-serving teacher and staff representative from the common room with a reputation for loudmouthing and bullying behaviour demanded to see him. The headmaster asked how he might be of assistance. The old-timer, who was a staff governor and thus fully aware of the school's financial predicament, revealed his intentions to retire in two years and demanded for his salary to be greatly increased so as to improve his pension pot – a practice which was commonplace under the previous headmaster, who governed by appeasement. "On what grounds should it be increased?" asked the new headmaster. The reply astounded him: "Because if you don't I can make life very difficult for you." Needless to say, the teacher was shown the door. The headmaster then recounted the incident to the staff in the common room without revealing the identity of the teacher. Standing firm in such situations is not always easy. The fear of what might happen if we do stand firm sometimes obscures our view of what we know is the right thing to do. It is, in the short term, easier to go with the flow, to fit in rather than do what is right and proper. We need the virtue of courage in our lives so that we can be true to ourselves. It gives us a framework on which to build lives which are true, good, compassionate, loving and fair.

If you were the new headmaster, what would you do?

a) Agree to enhance the bully's salary as long as he kept it quiet?

b) Laugh off his threats, stand firm and refuse his demands?

c) Try to explain to him the financial situation and the importance of keeping the business afloat to protect everyone's jobs?

d) Start proceedings against him for intimidation and harassment to send a message to others that you will not be bullied or harassed?

Remaining self-assured and unmoved by the bully's behaviour – no matter how insulting or intemperate it might be – shifts the focus of attention back onto the bully. It takes the sting out of their venom. Most bullies are one-dimensional and when their bullying behaviour is ineffective it throws them off kilter. Remember bullies feed on fear and when we no longer fear them we are not such an easy target for them to aim at.

Being strong and temperate in the face of intimidation takes courage. It requires strength of mind and of character. Like all good habits, being courageous takes effort and time to form, to grow and to inculcate within our lives. But it is worth it. Fiction and films often hold up the strong, silent type as a hero, someone to look up to and to aspire to be like. We admire their way of doing things. We want to be like them.

We want to be self-assured and self-possessed. We want to be our own person, calm and in control in the face of whatever adversities life might throw before us. Bullying prevents us from being the person we want to be. It inhibits us and reduces our ambitions and hopes to nothing. It takes courage to stand up to bullies, but it is the only response which will, ultimately, stop them. They feed off weakness and fear.

The virtue of temperance – *this allows us to restrain some of our wayward desires and passions and keeps them under control in difficult and trying situations.*

But being courageous is not the same as being brave. Walking away from a bully might not win awards or commendations for bravery, but in reality not responding in kind to their insults and threats is courageous. It takes guts to do so, to turn the other cheek when we feel angered or annoyed. This is why we need the virtue of temperance in our lives. Temperance keeps us on the straight and narrow path. It is the "still, calm voice" of reason within us, counselling us and guiding us wisely through difficult times. Of course, being temperate goes against the grain in our materialistic and possession-obsessed society. "Same day deliveries", "click and collect" and "instant credit" are the siren slogans and distinguishing features of modern life. They encourage us to believe we can have whatever we desire and that whatever we desire is worth having – until the next must-have product hits the high street, and then we desire that rather than the thing we desired before.

When bullies goad and torment, they are hoping for a reaction, something into which they can sink their hooks. There is nothing to be gained from rising to their bait – even if it seems, at the time, the natural thing to do so. Remaining resolute in one's belief that such behaviour is always and at all times wrong is the only course of action to take. Let this temper any thoughts and desires to respond in kind.

Bullies need to be in control. They thrive on being the dominant force in any relationship, situation or encounter. For the bully to keep hold of their control and maintain their dominance a victim must react in a way which is both predictable and normal to them. Bullies are not prepared or able to deal with reactions which are unexpected or out of the ordinary. They bank on the fact that their victim will cower and succumb to their dominance. This is why they have chosen the victim in the first place. They have sensed vulnerability or seen traits, mannerisms, idiosyncrasies or weaknesses which they can exploit to their own advantage. There is nothing random or casual about their behaviour. They only go after those whom they know they can bully.

As an experienced teacher I found it relatively easy to identify within a group the child who was more likely than their peers to be bullied. The same is true of the workplace. You only have one opportunity to make a first impression with a potential bully and it has to be the right one. The following incident illustrates my point. A family friend had recently been appointed to a new position and, after she had accepted the job, one of the interviewers let slip that she would be sharing an office with a "bit of a bully". An understatement. The woman was a very accomplished and successful bully with an alarming track record of having seen off a string of other colleagues. She was a serial bully but the management had never dealt with her. Our friend, a gentle soul and a thoroughly decent person, was, understandably, nervous on her first morning at the prospect of encountering the office bully, but she had already decided on a course of action. The old adage "to be forewarned is to be forearmed" was at the forefront of her thoughts and plans as she contemplated her first day at the office. She arrived intentionally early so that she was there to welcome the bully rather than the other way round – she was controlling the space, marking her area. When the bully arrived, our friend asked coolly and politely what she would like to drink. "Tea, strong and no sugar," she snapped, thrusting her mug in a threatening manner at her. In the bully's mind she believed it was business as usual, that her reputation had gone before her and here was another subservient minion for her to control and to bully as she saw fit. Our friend steeled herself and announced confidently, "Well, while you're at the kettle I'll have a coffee, white and no sugar." Here, using a simple and everyday act of making a brew and without any overt show of strength or aggression, she had asserted her presence and imposed her character on the bully.

If you were the new employee, what would you do?

a) Refuse to take up the position on hearing what the interviewer had let slip about the bully?

b) Go in with all (metaphorical) guns blazing and have a confrontation with the bully?

c) Keep your head down and just get on with the job until you have found something else?

d) Try to appease the bully?

e) Assert your authority in a quiet and unobtrusive manner so the bully quickly realises you cannot be bullied?

Needless to say, from that day on the bully was back in her box.

Being confident, positive and self-possessed are all behaviours that deter bullies. Lacking confidence and showing timidity and reticence are positive signs of encouragement for many bullies. A temperate character – not overly assertive or loudly confident – is the ideal. Strength is not about exerting power and dominance over others or flexing one's muscle. A strong, self-assured person is temperate and confident in the knowledge that they are in control of their own lives – including their emotions, desires and appetites. If a bully cannot exert power, then there is nothing else in their repertoire.

Bullies will latch on to anything which empowers them. A relatively new phenomenon is "financial bullying". When partners separate often they remain tied together financially, with house, pensions and other assets owned jointly. More often than not it is the mother who tends to have custody of children, but regrettably some bullies use this to exploit their spouses and to continue to control them by controlling their financial means to properly care for the children. Only government intervention and legislation can put a stop to this abuse.

The virtue of justice – this virtue involves respecting others and fulfilling our obligations to them, in spite of what we might feel about them or think of them.

One of the many points about Jesus' teaching in the Gospels is how it differs radically from the teaching of the Pharisees – the Jewish leaders and teachers. He heals people on the Sabbath. He puts people first, not the observance of rules and regulations. Similarly, he does not condemn to death the woman caught in the act of adultery, as the bloodthirsty and seemingly righteous mob had wanted him to do. He tells her to go away and not to sin again. He spends time with those who have been shunned by society as outcasts and sinners. In spite of what the Pharisees or the baying mob might feel or think, Jesus continues to act justly. When others have sinned he maintains his respect for them. He does not allow their sins or their wrongdoing to detract from or reduce his love for them. Even in his final agonising moments on the cross he asks his heavenly father to forgive those who have crucified him. Jesus never loses sight of his obligation to others. He never gives up on them. It is a hard path to follow but not an impossible one if we remain steadfast in a belief that justice matters.

Bullies do not stop being temples of the Holy Spirit or lose their unique imprint as having been made in the image and likeness of God because of their behaviour – no matter how much we may disapprove of it. Their sacredness is inviolable. It can, at times, be obscured, swamped by their destructive behaviour and mind-set, but it never diminishes, never leaves them. The challenge here is to act justly and to set the bully back on the right path without diminishing or condoning the damage they have undoubtedly caused to another person and to the wider community. This means that both bully and victim are helped equally, even if this does not sit easily with others. Justice demands it.

All too often with bullying in the workplace the real issues are not resolved but instead, more often than not, the victim or the bully is simply moved on. This is not justice because it fails to uphold a duty of care to give to each what is fair and necessary. It's worth remembering that sometimes a bully's behaviour might be an unrecognised and unspoken cry for help in coping with his or her own pain.

- Joan said of her grandfather, "He didn't start off as a bully: he became one. He was twenty and a junior crew member on an iron sailing barque which was shipwrecked in Vivero Bay, off the coast of Mexico, in May 1906. Three months later, on another ship, he was in Valparaiso Harbour during the 1906 earthquake, one of the biggest in recorded history. He and his shipmates went ashore to help with the burials. Eight years later, now in the Merchant Navy, he sailed through World War I. Later, as a master mariner and in various senior positions – including captain – again in the Merchant Navy, he sailed through World War II, was part of the Arctic Convoy, rescued the crew of a sinking lifeboat in Arctic waters and ignored the 'experts' who said it was impossible to take his ship into Odessa to bring troops home after the war. If you remember, one-third of the crews of Merchant Navy ships were killed during World War II. He lost so many people he knew. He watched ships go down. After the war, the ocean-going passenger liner of which he was to take command caught fire and burned down in dry dock. It could have happened at sea. My grandfather was decorated for his outstanding courage, but it took its toll on him. He had taken command for most of his life because other people's lives depended on his decision-making. Post-Traumatic Stress Disorder (PTSD) wasn't known then and so he got out of the habit of negotiating and dialogue. His orders – even to the family – required instant obedience. If he could have been helped, he wouldn't have been a bully. Sadly, he died before PTSD was recognised and support became available. In spite of his bullying, he and my grandmother idolised each other: he just couldn't see that he was the one who needed to change."

- Kate discovered that tragedy underpinned the bullying behaviour of one of her patients. "John was extraordinarily difficult. I was assigned to look after him because I was a student nurse. Everybody else gave up on him. After a few days, as I was helping him to wash and dress, he suddenly burst into tears. It turned out that his first wife had died of cancer after only three years of a very happy marriage.

He married again and his second wife also died, leaving him with two children, whom he brought up on his own. A short time before John was admitted to hospital, his son, discovering that he also had cancer, found a gun and shot himself through the mouth. 'I know I'm difficult,' John sobbed, 'but I just can't take any more.' Following his outburst, John was a much easier patient: he'd needed an outlet for his pain and anger. Until he managed to cry and tell his story, he had lashed out at everybody."

Both sides of the story

Employers, managers or whoever is in authority have an obligation to both parties – the bullied and the bully. If they merely relocate one or both of the individuals, they simply move the problem on to another workplace. Such expedients might, in the short term, be beneficial to the business or institution, but employers need to be mindful of the fact that they have a wider responsibility for their staff, a part to play beyond their own business interests and profits.

Just as they must be aware of and demonstrate their ethical responsibility for their impact on the environment – their "carbon footprint" – so too must they be mindful of their moral impact on the wider community. They have a duty not only to trade fairly and ethically with others, but also to evaluate their behaviour towards their own employees. Do they treat them justly? Do they give their employees what they are entitled to? In the case of bullying, how do they care for the bully's victims and for the bully? What provisions do they have in place to ensure that there are no practices or pressures applied from the top down on managers which might permit the formation of a bullying culture within their workplace, or allow it to be ignored?

If managers or supervisors bully their staff with impunity, it is often because they are following directives from above which, implicitly or explicitly, legitimise and condone such behaviour. Where profits are put before the welfare and well-being of staff, there can be no justice in these workplaces. In this toxic environment, many managers and supervisors will be quick to take advantage of a so-called bullying culture and use it to advance their own career and personal ambitions. Justice demands that people are only appointed to roles of authority if they can demonstrate integrity and an ability to be just with all those they are in charge of regardless of how they might feel or think about a particular individual.

Being just does not permit or allow us to "pass the buck", leaving the problem for someone else further down the line to deal with. Every society, community and workplace needs all of its people, its entire workforce in the case of a company, working together constructively and harmoniously for the benefit of the whole. If there is a culture of bullying, this cannot happen. While the bullies work selfishly for their own ends and not for the common good, their victims are prevented from flourishing and contributing their God-given talents and natural attributes to the well-being of the whole.

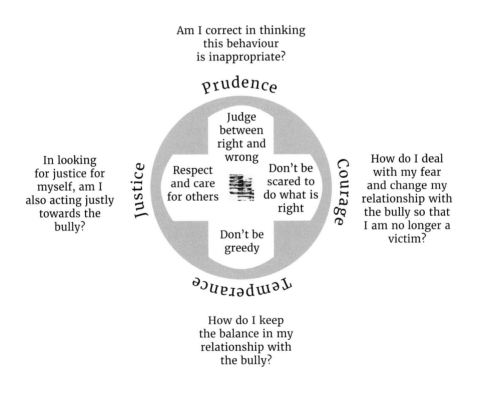

Am I correct in thinking
this behaviour
is inappropriate?

prudence

Judge
between
right and
wrong

In looking
for justice for
myself, am I
also acting justly
towards the
bully?

Justice

Respect
and care
for others

Don't be
scared to
do what is
right

Courage

How do I deal
with my fear
and change my
relationship with
the bully so that
I am no longer a
victim?

Don't be
greedy

Temperance

How do I keep
the balance in my
relationship with
the bully?

"We explain when someone is cruel or acts like a bully, you do not stoop to their level. Our motto is when they go low, you go high."

Michelle Obama

7

In summary

If, as former Prime Minister David Cameron has said, stamping out bullying in the workplace and elsewhere is a "vital objective", then we will need a strategic and all-inclusive approach to the scourge of bullying. Focusing on the four cardinal virtues – prudence, courage, temperance and justice – will go a long way to providing such an approach. In utilitarian and practical terms it provides clear and quantifiable evidence. Keeping the cardinal virtues firmly in mind allows us to ask the following questions about the staff in a workplace: Do people act prudently? Do they show courage? Are they temperate? Do people act justly with others? If we can test and assess a business in terms of its productivity and financial health, then surely we can do the same when it comes to looking at how people in the workforce behave and interact with each other?

To do so, we will need the virtue of prudence to judge what we are doing right and what we are not doing right in terms of how we run and oversee our places of work.

We will need the virtue of courage to overcome the fear and anxiety relating to self-examination and scrutiny which will inevitably result from our examination of ourselves and how we think, act and behave towards each other.

We will need the virtue of temperance to help us to remain balanced and dispassionate as we seek to discern the right and proper path to take.

We will need the virtue of justice to ensure that we do what is right and proper for all people and for society as a whole when dealing with bullies and bullying behaviour in the workplace.

8

Prayers and meditations

The serenity prayer

> God grant me the serenity
> to accept the things I cannot change;
> courage to change the things I can;
> and wisdom to know the difference.

Reinhold Niebuhr (1892–1971)

Meditation: love is all you need

If I speak in the tongues of mortals and of angels, but do not have love, I am a noisy gong or a clanging cymbal… Love is patient; love is kind; love is not envious or boastful or arrogant or rude. It does not insist on its own way; it is not irritable or resentful; it does not rejoice in wrongdoing, but rejoices in the truth. It bears all things, believes all things, hopes all things, endures all things… And now faith, hope, and love abide, these three; and the greatest of these is love.

(1 Corinthians 13:1-13)

Prayer/meditation: give peace a chance

Make me a channel of your peace.
Where there is hatred let me bring love;
Where there is despair in life let me bring hope;
Where there is darkness only light
And where there is sadness, ever joy.
Make me a channel of your peace.

(From the Prayer of Saint Francis)

Meditation: the inward struggle

I do not understand my own actions. For I do not do what I want,
but I do the very thing I hate… So I find it to be a law that when
I want to do what is good, evil lies close at hand.

(Romans 7:15–21)

Meditation: the other person

If the other person laughs at you, you can pity him; but if you
laugh at him you may never forgive yourself.

If the other person injures you, you may forget the injury;
but if you injure him you will always remember.

In truth the other person is your most sensitive self
given another body.

(From Kahlil Gibran, Sand and Foam)

Meditation: getting under the skin of things

Atticus stood up and walked to the end of the porch. When he completed his examination of the wisteria vine he strolled back to me.

"First of all," he said, "if you can learn a simple trick, Scout, you'll get along a lot better with all kinds of folks. You never really understand a person until you consider things from his point of view—"

"Sir?"

"—until you climb into his skin and walk around in it."

(From Harper Lee, To Kill a Mockingbird)

Meditation: keep calm and carry on

Let no evil talk come out of your mouths, but only what is useful for building up, as there is need, so that your words may give grace to those who hear... Put away from you all bitterness and wrath and anger and wrangling and slander, together with all malice, and be kind to one another, tenderhearted, forgiving one another, as God in Christ has forgiven you.

(Ephesians 4:29-32)

Meditation: to love and to reconcile

... not to judge, not to be superior, not to exercise power, not to seek, seek, seek. To love and to reconcile and to forgive, only this matters... Love is the only justice.

(From Iris Murdoch, The Nice and The Good)

Meditation: word betraying the heart

Either make the tree good, and its fruit good; or make the tree bad, and its fruit bad; for the tree is known by its fruit... For out of the abundance of the heart the mouth speaks. The good person brings good things out of a good treasure, and the evil person brings evil things out of an evil treasure.

(Matthew 12:33–36)

Lectio Divina

Lectio Divinia (from the Latin "Divine Reading") is a traditional Benedictine practice of using a passage of scripture to reflect on and to meditate and to pray. Passages of scripture can be used to help us reflect on how we behave, how we relate to other people. The parable of the Good Samaritan in the Gospel of Luke can be a useful passage to examine such issues with a group or an individual.

After each extract I will suggest ways in which it might be used.

The context of the parable

Jesus is responding to a lawyer who has asked him how he might inherit eternal life. Jesus asks him, "What is written in the Law?" The man replied, "You shall love the Lord your God with all your heart, and with all your soul, and with all your strength, and with all your mind; and your neighbour as yourself." Jesus told the man he had answered correctly and then told him to "do this, and you will live".

The parable of the Good Samaritan: Luke 10:29–34

But wanting to justify himself, he asked Jesus, "And who is my neighbour?"

- The man seems to know what to do to have eternal life. He knows the Law requires him to love his neighbour, yet he asks, "Who is my neighbour?"

- Is it possible to love someone we do not know?

- What does it mean "to love your neighbour as yourself"?

- Who is my neighbour?

Jesus replied, "A man was going down from Jerusalem to Jericho, and fell into the hands of robbers, who stripped him, beat him, and went away, leaving him half dead. Now by chance a priest was going down that road; and when he saw him, he passed by on the other side. So likewise a Levite, when he came to the place and saw him, passed by on the other side.

- How do you feel about the priest and the Levite?

- Why do you think they passed by the man?

- What should they have done for the man?

- Why?

- What would you have done if you were in their place?

- What stopped them from doing the right thing and helping the man?

But a Samaritan while travelling came near him; and when he saw him, he was moved with pity. He went to him and bandaged his wounds, having poured oil and wine on them. Then he put him on his own animal, brought him to an inn, and took care of him."

- Why do you think the Samaritan stopped to help the man?

- Is it not easier to leave the man, just as the priest and the Levite had done?

- Why should the Samaritan get involved?

- Would you have stopped or passed by on the other side?

- Which of these three do you think loved his neighbour?